KU-360-216

This copy of

JOKES FROM OUTER SPACE

belongs to

JOHN A J MUIR

Ruth

JOKES FROM OUTER SPACE

KATIE WALES

Illustrated by Mark Burgess

Beaver Books

A Beaver Book
Published by Arrow Books Limited
62–5 Chandos Place, London WC2N 4NW

An imprint of Century Hutchinson Ltd

London Melbourne Sydney Auckland
Johannesburg and agencies throughout the world

First published 1987

Set in Century Schoolbook
by JH Graphics Ltd, Reading

Made and printed in Great Britain
by Anchor Brendon Ltd
Tiptree, Essex

ISBN 09 945290 1

for Tim – again

Contents

Count Down

What did the computer say to the programmer?
'You can count on me.'

What do you get if you cross the sea with a computer?
A brain-wave.

What's the best way to count cows?
With a cow-culator.

What do you get if you cross a computer with a boat?
A rowbot.

What do you get if you cross a computer with an elephant?
A two-ton know-all.

What did one computer say to the other?
'I've got lots of problems.'

Did you hear about the Irish scientist who covered his VDU with Tippex?

What did the robot say when it ran out of electricity?
'AC come, AC go.'

What car do robots drive?
A Volts-wagon.

What did the robot say to his girlfriend?
'I love you watts and watts.'

What did the girlfriend say to the robot?
'You're so electrocute.'

Why did the robot go mad?
Because it had a screw loose.

What's a robot's nearest relation?
A trans-sister.

What's a robot's favourite meal?
Silicon-chips.

What happened to the robot who ate too much?
It got atomic-ache.

What did the mother robot say to the little robot at midnight?
'Wire you insulate?'

Where do robots fight?
In a scrapyard.

What kind of jokes did Einstein make?
Wise-cracks.

Why did the robot grease his joints before going to bed?
Because he wanted to get up oily in the morning.

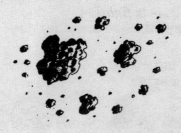

What was the scientist's reaction when he discovered electricity?
He was shocked.

What do scientists do on holiday?
They go fission.

Who is a scientist's favourite poet?
Robot Burns.

Who is a scientist's favourite actor?
Robot de Niro.

Did you hear about the computer that broke down?
The doctor diagnosed metal fatigue.

Sign seen at Ground Control at lunch-time:
'Gone for a byte'.

What do you get if you cross a germ with a potato?
A microbe-chip.

What do you call a robot that eats too much?
Heavy Metal.

How does a robot stand?
Bolt upright.

If space scientists are so clever, why do they count backwards?

And Lift-Off . . .

Why is a spaceship like a tramp?
They both have no visible means of support.

What kind of ears do spaceships have?
Engin-eers.

What does an astronaut do when he gets angry?
He blasts off.

What do you get if you cross a rocket with a kangaroo?
A space shuttle that makes short hops.

Did you hear about the nervous astronaut who asked Ground Control, 'Do rockets crash often?'
'Only once,' came the reply.

What's stupid and goes into space?
A loony module.

Did you hear about the spaceship that was so old it had an outside toilet?

What did the hijacker say to the astronaut?
'Fly me to the moon . . .'

Who was the first animal in space?
The cow who jumped over the moon.

What goes 'MOOZ...'
An upside-down rocket.

*What is yellow and goes up and down at
1000 mph?*
A banana in a rocket.

What goes up and never comes down?
Your age.

Who was the first man in space?
The man in the moon.

Why doesn't the sea fall into space?
Because it's tide (tied).

What do you call an astronaut who's afraid of heights?
A failure.

What is the centre of gravity?
The letter 'V'.

Why can't elephants fly in space?
Because their trunks won't fit under the seat.

One astronaut said to another astronaut: 'Just look at those people down there, they just look like ants.'
'They are ants,' the other said. 'We've not left the launch-pad yet.'

What is an astronaut's favourite meal?
Launch.

What do astronauts get if they do their calculations properly?
Gold stars.

Did you hear about the Irish astronauts who planned to fly to the sun? Of course, they knew it was hot – so they decided to go at night.

Sign seen at Ground Control at blast-off:
'Watch this space'.

It was Wally's first trip in space. 'What happens if we run out of rocket-fuel?' he asked his co-pilot.
'We get out and push', answered Fred.

'Look at that speed,' said one eagle to another, as a spaceship flew overhead.
'So would *you* be fast,' said the other, 'if your tail was on fire!'

What did the astronaut say as he kissed his wife good-bye?
'Must fly now.'

Astronuts . . .

What astronaut is always in a hurry?
A Russian.

What does an astronaut do when he's dirty?
Has a meteor shower.

Where do astronauts park their spaceships?
On meter-ites.

If an athlete gets athlete's foot, what does an astronaut get?
Missile-toe

What should an astronaut never do?
Look down.

What illness do astronauts suffer from?
Flu. (Geddit?)

What astronaut wears the biggest helmet?
The one with the biggest head.

How do astronauts keep warm?
They wear Apollo-neck jumpers.

What do astronauts suffer from if they sit down too long?
Asteroids.

What do astronauts play football on?
Astro-turf.

What do you call a space-prison?
A sput-nick.

Why is a prisoner like an astronaut?
They're both keen on outer space.

Paddy and Mick were the first Irishmen in space. Paddy set off on a space walk, leaving Mick in charge of the spaceship. An hour later he heard a 'knock knock' on the hatch. 'Who's there?' he asked.

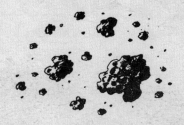

What is an astronaut's favourite snack?
Mars bars.

What's an astronaut's favourite game?
Astro-noughts and crosses.

What did the two astronauts say to St Peter at the Pearly Gates?
'Please, sir, can we have our satellite back?'

What books do astronauts like to read?
Star Wars by Ronald Ray-gun
Astrology by Horace Cope
Space Invaders by I. C. Marshan and Ann Droid
Splitting the Atom by Molly Cule
Astronomy by I. C. Stars
Space Travel by Count Down
Moon Landings by Willie Makeit

Can you telephone from a spaceship?
Of course I can tell a phone from a
spaceship . . .

What do you call an astronaut's watch?
A lunar-tick.

What do you call a crazy space-man?
An astro-nut.

How do you get a baby astronaut to fall asleep?
You rock-et.

What do you get if you cross a skunk with an astronaut?
An animal that stinks to high heaven.

How do astronauts play badminton?
With space shuttles.

Star Wars . . .

What's black and silly and appears in Star Wars?
Daft Vader.

What does Luke Skywalker shave with?
A laser blade.

Why did Darth Vader turn down streaky bacon from the butchers?
Because the Empire likes back.

What happens when the cow who jumped over the moon meets Taurus the Bull?
Steer wars.

What do you get if you cross Darth Vader with a cricket referee?
The Umpire Strikes Back.

Who is big and hairy and smells?
Phew-Bacca.

What do you get if you cross a planet with a toad?
Star warts.

What do you call wobbly invaders?
Return of the Jelly.

What's purple and flies in outer space?
The Planet of the Grapes.

How do you get to the Planet of the Apes?
By banana boat.

'Waiter, waiter, there's a strange film on my soup.'
'What do you expect for 50p – 2001?'

What does Mr Spock eat for breakfast?
Star brek.

What's another name for a space-walk?
A star trek.

How many ears has Captain Kirk?
Three: the left ear, the right ear, and the final
frontier.

Two men wanted to audition for a part in
Star Trek. The first man had pointed ears, so
he wanted to play Spock; the second man was
dressed as a tree.
'What part do you want?' asked the producer,
puzzled. 'The Captain's log,' he replied.

What do you call a beetle from space?
Bug Rogers.

Knock, knock.
Who's there?
Doctor.
Doctor who?
That's right . . .

What is a kangaroo's favourite TV
programme?
Dr Roo.

What is a cow's favourite TV programme?
Dr Moo.

Where does K9 go for his holidays?
Pluto.

Where does K9 live?
The dog-star.

What is written on a Dalek's tombstone?
Rust in Peace.

Super-Heroes . . .

Knock, knock.
Who's there?
Soup.
Soup who?
Souperman.

Why does Superman have big shoes?
Because of his amazing feats.

Where does Superman buy his breakfast
cereal?
At the supermarket, of course.

What's green and flies around the world?
Super-pickle.

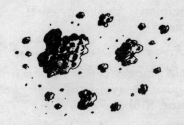

What's red and blue and drunk and flies
around the world?
Stuporman.

What's black and white and flies around the
world?
Supernun.

What super-hero would be good at cricket?
Batman.

Why isn't Batman married?
Because he's a bat-chelor.

What is Batman's favourite sport?
Bat-minton.

What would you get if Batman and Robin were trampled on by a herd of elephants?
Flatman and Ribbon.

*What would you get if Batman and Robin
were trampled on by a herd of stampeding
buffaloes?*
The Mashed Crusaders.

*What did Batman's mother say when she
wanted him to come him for lunch?*
'Dinner-dinner-dinner-dinner, dinner-dinner-
dinner-dinner, BATMAN . . .'

Why couldn't Batman go fishing?
Because Robin ate all the worms.

*Why does Batman brush his teeth at least
three times day?*
To prevent bat (bad) breath.

What was Batman doing up the tree?
Looking for Robin's nest.

Why did Batman go to the pet shop?
To buy a Robin.

What was Batman doing in the sky?
Aerobatics.

What does Spiderman do when he gets angry?
He goes up the wall.

What's green, seven feet tall and sits in a corner?
The Incredible Sulk.

What is eight feet tall, green and wrinkly?
The Incredible Hulk's granny.

What do you get if you cross a pen with an elephant?
The Ink-credible Hulk.

*What do you call the Incredible Hulk with a
banana in each ear?*
Anything – he can't hear you!

What do you call the Incredible Hulk with BO?
The great smell of Brut . . .

What's red and runs in slow motion?
The bionic nose.

What happens when a bionic baby is born?
Nothing – the doctor's afraid to smack it.

Did you hear about the bionic man who was caught speeding on the M1? He was fined £100 and dismantled for twelve months.

What is long and green, has one bionic eye, and fights crime?
The Six-Million-Dollar Cucumber.

Did you hear about the man who thought the Rover 2000 was a bionic dog?

Why did the Invisible Man look in the mirror?
Because he wanted to see if he still wasn't
there.

What did one Invisible Man say to another?
'It's nice not to see you again.'

PATIENT: *I keep feeling like the Invisible Man.*
DOCTOR: Who said that?

What is more invisible than the Invisible Man?
His shadow.

SECRETARY: *The Invisible Man is waiting to*
see you.
DOCTOR: Tell him I can't see him.

What does the Invisible Man call his Mum
and Dad?
His transparents.

What did the Invisible Girl want to be when she grew up?
A gone-gone dancer.

What is the Invisible Man's favourite drink?
Evaporated milk.

Why did the Invisible Man go mad?
Out of sight, out of mind.

What's big, hairy and can fly at Mach two?
King Kongcorde.

Why did King Kong play with the flying saucer?
He thought it was a frisbee.

Why did King Kong climb Cleopatra's Needle?
To get his kite back.

*What did King Kong say when he saw the
Statue of Liberty?*
'Hello, Mum.'

*Why did King Kong climb up the Empire State
Building?*
To catch a plane.

*If King Kong went to Hong Kong and played
ping-pong and died, what would they put on
his coffin?*
A lid?

*What do you get if you cross King Kong with a
bell?*
A ding-dong King Kong.

*How did you like the story of the Abominable
Snowman?*
It left me cold.

Knock, knock.
Who's there?
Dan Dare
Dan Dare who?
Dan Dare is de big hole

Knock, knock.
Who's there?
Frank.
Frank who?
Frankenstein.

Why was Frankenstein never lonely?
He was good at making friends.

Who brings monsters their babies?
Frankenstork.

*Why did the girlfriend of Frankenstein's
monster break up with him?*
Because he had a crush on her.

What did Frankenstein's monster say when a
bolt of lightning struck him?
'Thanks, I needed that!'

How did Frankenstein make his monster
laugh?
He had him in stitches.

What was Dr Jekyll's favourite game?
Hyde and Shriek.

Close Encounters ...

How many letters are there in the alphabet?
Twenty-two since JR was shot and ET went home.

What do you call a fat ET?
An extra-cholesterol.

What is ET's favourite year?
19 ET 3. *(1983)*

What did ET's mother say to him when he came in for tea?
'Where on earth have you been?'

What's small and brown and travels at 100 m.p.h?
ET on a motor bike.

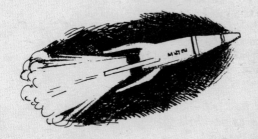

Why did ET get a shock?
Because he'd just received his phone bill.

What alien has the best hearing?
The eeriest.

What do you call an alien who talks through his nose?
An adenoid.

What do you call an alien who thinks he's being followed?
A paranoid.

What did the astronauts say about the eight-legged aliens?
'Don't worry, they're arm-less.'

What has a purple-spotted body, ten hairy legs, and eyes on stalks?
I don't know.
Nor do I, but there's one crawling up your back . . .

What are space fleas called?
Lunar-tics.

What do you call a space insect?
An astro-gnat.

What do you call a flea that lives in an idiot's ear?
A space invader.

What did the alien say to his girlfriend?
'I wanna hold your hand, hand, hand . . .'

What did she say to him?
'I believe in love at first fright.'

How do aliens drink tea?
Out of flying saucers.

Where do aliens park their flying saucers?
At parking meteors.

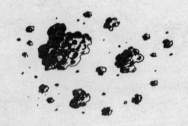

What would you say if you met a three-headed alien?
'Hello, hello, hello.'

How does an alien count to fifteen?
On its fingers.

What steps would you take if you had a close encounter with an alien?
Large ones – in the opposite direction!

Why are aliens forgetful?
Because everything goes in one ear and out the others.

What do you call a one-eyed monster on a motor bike?
Cycle-ops.

How does an alien impress people?
It puts its beast foot forward.

The Martians have landed . . .

What is soft, white and sweet and comes from Mars?
Martian-mallows.

What did the Martian say to the petrol pump?
'Take your finger out of your ear and listen to what I'm saying.'

When are soldiers like aliens?
When they're Martian along.

Did you hear about the two Martians who
landed near a pillar-box. 'Take me to your
leader,' one said to it.
'Don't be silly,' said the other. 'Can't you see
it's only a child?'

*What did the Martian say when he landed in
a flower-bed?*
'Take me to your weeder.'

Did you hear about the two Martians who
landed near a traffic-light. 'I saw her first,'
said one.
'Well, I'm the one she winked at,' retorted the
other.

*What did the Martian say when he landed on
Brighton beach?*
'Take me to your Lido.'

Did you hear about the Martian who landed on earth, and the first person he met was a woman with a transistor radio?
He told her off for carrying her child around with no clothes on!

Two Martians landed near a large town. Pointing to the TV aerials one said to the other, grinning, 'Look at all those lovely girls!'

What is the best way to talk to a Martian?
By long distance.

Where does a Martian sleep?
Anywhere it wants to.

What is woolly, covered in chocolate, and goes round the sun?
A Mars baaa.

Who is the President of Mars?
Ronald Ray-gun.

What do you say when a Martian walks up to you with a laser-gun?
I give up.
That's right . . .

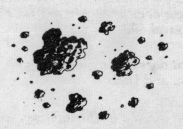

A space-ship with two Martians crash-landed on Earth.
'We'll never get back home,' said one. 'What are we going to do? Our engines are all smashed.'
'Don't worry,' replied the pilot. 'We'll think of something. After all, four heads are better than one.'

Two Martians landed on earth, and one went off to explore. He came back and took his friend to see the sights. They came to a pillar-box and a telephone kiosk.
'That little red fellow has nothing to say for himself,' he told his friend. 'He just stares with his mouth open. But watch out for the bigger one: when you get near him he sneezes his head off.'

What does a baby Martian call its parents?
Mum and Dad.

What did the traffic-light say to the Martian?
'Don't look now, I'm changing.'

What did the man say when he trod on a bar of chocolate?
'I've set foot on Mars.'

What is better than presence of mind when a Martian aims his laser-gun?
Absence of body.

Unidentified flying objects . . .

What did the astronaut see in his saucepan?
An unidentified frying object.

What is a pie in the sky?
A flying pizza.

What flies and wobbles?
A jellycopter.

What dish is out of this world?
A flying saucer.

What's yellow and hovers over the kitchen?
An unidentified frying omelette.

What is long and yellow and travels great distances?
An inter-continental banana missile.

What skims over the water and barks at cats?
Hovercrufts.

What flies around the earth gabbling about the stars?
Sputnik Moore.

What do you call a flying St Paul's Cathedral?
An aerodome.

What do you call a witch on a broomstick?
A flying sorcerer.

What's long and orange and flies at the speed of sound?
A jet-propelled carrot.

What is the best way to see flying saucers?
Trip up a waiter.

How does a bird land in an emergency?
By sparrow-chute.

Who didn't invent the aeroplane?
The Wrong Brothers.

What's blue and yellow with a fourteen-metre wing span?
A two-and-a-half-ton budgie.

What do you eat somewhere over the rainbow?
A way up pie.

What pies can fly?
Magpies.

*What do you get if you cross the white of an
egg with a pound of gunpowder?*
A boom-meringue.

*What do you get if you cross a helicopter with
a shark?*
A helichopper.

What has twenty-two legs and two wings but can't fly?
A football team.

How do toads fly?
By hoppercraft.

What do you call a flying policeman?
A helicopper.

Moon madness . . .

What holds the moon up?
Moon-beams.

How do you arrange a trip to the moon?
Plan-et.

When can't astronauts land on the moon?
When it's full.

How did the cow jump over the moon?
She followed the Milky Way.

Did you hear about the astronauts who played football in the first ever football match in space?
The winners were over the moon.

What happened when the cow jumped over the moon?
The price of milk rocketed.

Hey Diddle Diddle
The cat and the fiddle,
The cow blew up
On the launching pad.

Hey Diddle Diddle
The cat and the fiddle,
The cow jumped over the moon
And burned up on re-entry.

Did you hear about the astronaut who opened the first pub on the moon?
It wasn't a success: people said it lacked atmosphere.

How did Mary's little lamb get to the moon?
By rocket sheep.

Which is more important, the sun or the moon?
The moon. It shines when it's dark, but the sun shines when it's light anyway.

Why are there no dogs on the moon?
Because there are no trees on the moon.

Two little moonmen sat staring at the earth
shining in the sky.
'Do you think there's life on earth?' asked one.
'Oh yes,' replied the other. 'They're probably
sitting around just like us, nibbling rocks.'

When is the moon heaviest?
When it's full.

Seeing stars . . .

What did the big star say to the little star?
'You're too young to stay out at night.'

When is a window like a star?
When it's a sky-light.

Why is Lassie like Halley's comet?
They're both stars with tails.

What stars go to prison?
Shooting stars.

What did one shooting star say to the other?
'Pleased to meteor.'

What is the dog star?
Lassie.

Name a shooting star.
Clint Eastwood.

Why are false teeth like stars?
They come out at night.

What kind of person watches the stars?
A cinema addict.

What goes on in a planetarium?
An all-star show.

What kind of star wears sun-glasses?
A film star.

Which is the noisiest planet?
Saturn, because it has so many rings.

*What do Mars, Galaxy and the Milky Way
have in common?*
They are all chocolate bars.

What swim in space?
Starfish.

Who settled in the West before anyone else?
The sun.

How do you phone the sun?
Use a sun-dial.

Did you hear about the Irishman who sat up all night wondering where the sun had gone?
The next morning it dawned on him.

Why do astronauts wear bullet-proof suits?
To protect themselves from shooting stars.

*What is the difference between the sun and a
loaf of bread?*
One rises from the east and the other from
the yeast.

What is lighter, the sun or the earth?
The sun – it rises every morning.

Knock, knock.
Who's there?
Star.
Star who?
Starsky and Hutch.

Knock, knock.
Who's there?
Jupiter.
Jupiter who?
Jupiter go home now.

Why did the astronomer hit himself on the head?
Because he wanted to see stars.

Knock, knock.
Who's there?
Saturn.
Saturn who?
Saturnight Fever.

Knock, knock.
Who's there?
Mars.
Mars who?
Marsock's got a hole in it.

What is more nourishing, a cow or a shooting star?
A star because it is meteor. (Geddit?)

Where are starfish found?
In a planet-arium.

How many balls of string would it take to reach Jupiter?
One, if it was long enough.

What is the difference between the rising and the setting sun?
A day.

What is the most musical planet?
Nep-tune.

Why is the letter 'G' like the sun?
Because they are both the centre of light.

What is an astronomer?
A night watchman with a good education.

Why is astronomy so popular?
Because it's a heavenly job.

Splash down . . .

*Who gets congratulated when they're down
and out?*
Astronauts.

Why did the astronaut crash into the house?
Because the landing lights were on.

Why is an astronaut like a baseball player?
They both want to make safe touch-downs.

*What is the beginning of eternity,
The end of time and space,
The beginning of every end,
And the end of every race?*
The letter 'E'.

Graffiti rules the universe – OK? . . .

E.T. — phone home

Have you seen the Invisible Man lately?

Yes

There's no future in Time travel

BEWARE LOW-FLYING PYGMIES

Keep the Pope off
the Moon—
It's the only place he
hasn't been!

BATMAN LOVES ROBIN

Isaac Newton was a down-to-
earth man

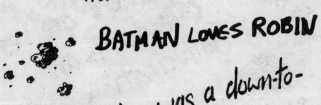

IS THERE INTELLIGENT LIFE
ON
EARTH?

Yes— but I'm only ~~Visting~~!
here weekends

IS THERE LIFE IN PECKHAM?

Is there life on Patrick Moore?

UFO's are real.

Neasden is an hallucination

ISAAC NEWTON WAS RIGHT—
THIS IS THE CENTRE OF GRAFFITI

EINSTEIN RULES—
RELATIVELY OK

If Batman is so smart, why
does he wear his underpants
OUTSIDE his trousers?

Say it with flowers—
Give her a Triffid

STOP THE WORLD
I WANT TO GET OFF

I've lived on vegetables all my life
That's nothing— I've lived on Earth!

You've never alone
with a clone

What keeps jazz musicians
on earth?
—Groovity!

For Sale: Space ship.
One Owner. Only
5, 000,000,000
            miles.